Can't they see what they do?

By Elise L. Walker

Edited by: Claude R. Royston

BK Royston Publishing LLC
Jeffersonville, IN

BK Royston Publishing
P. O. Box 4321
Jeffersonville, IN 47131
502-802-5385
http://bkroystonpublishing.com

Published by: BK Royston Publishing LLC
Cover Design by: Erick Bowen
Layout by: BK Royston Publishing LLC

ISBN-13: 978-0615908199

ISBN-10: 0615908195

Printed in the United States of America

Dedication

This book is dedicated to
My loving family
My husband
Fred
My awesome children
Christopher, Kimberly, April
And their spouses
Vanessa, Sam, Andre
And my seven grandchildren
Alexis
Michael Jr.
Regan
Jaden
Andre
Gabrielle
Kaden
And those to be born in
December 2013 and March 2014

Acknowledgements

Special thanks to the many sister/friends who encouraged me, prayed for me and allowed me to share with them from time to time some of the many writings God put on my heart to write.

Pam Allen
Sherry Austin
Lisa Banks
Deborah Barnwell
Lisa Betts
Bellvia Bonnafon
Mary Buford
Melinda Campbell
Nicole Curtis
Melissa Dawson
Janice Harris
Deloris House
Katherine Jones
Janice Johnson
Audrey Lee
Betty Macklin

Sherry Mattingly
Janice Miller
Marna Miller
Sandra Posey
Julia Royston
Arletta Shouse
Clydia Smith
Sha'Lethea Spencer
Lori Sperry
Donyce Spires
Angela Tellis
Helen Thomas
Cheryl Turner
Shiela Ulrich
Susan Walsh
Mary Webb
Sis. Annie White
Joann "Mother Sunshine" Williams
Roger Wilson
Teresa Williams
My Deer Park Sisters
My LabCorp Sisters

And a very special thanks to my Aunt
Brenda Jackson
that we all so lovingly call

Aunt Friday
she has always been in my life whenever I
have needed her.

Thank you so much for being there and
believing in me.

Dear Reader,

God is so awesome, if there is any doubt in your mind about our heavenly Father I am here to tell you that without Him I would not be writing these words. As a matter of fact, I would not even be alive to write these words. At one point in my life, I was ready to give up on life, depression, low self-esteem was just a few of my strongholds that I allowed to control me. God had blessed me with a beautiful family but I was allowing many things from my past childhood to cloud my joy and happiness. I am so thankful to God for changing my life and allowing me to not give up on life so that I may be used by God to be a blessing to someone else.

I am here to tell you that it matters not how your life starts out it only matters what you do with the life you are given. Yes, I would have loved to have had the perfect family life with a mother and father who would have loved me and raised me together along with my sisters and brothers. But that was not the way it was meant to be, so get over it. Wow that took me a lot of drinking, then therapy, and antidepressants to be able to say that, but the alcohol was leading me down a slippery slope to another kind of problem. When I got upset or my feelings got hurt or I just wanted to feel good I would drink. I was that closet binge drinker, no one had any idea how much alcohol I was putting away not even my husband.

Nothing changed until I really gave my life to Christ and allowed him to work on me to quit smoking cigarettes, stop drinking and to start forgiving those folks who had ever hurt me in the past. Nothing changed until I called on the Lord to help me be a better person, wife and mother. I have learned to forgive in my heart and mind. Until God, I was destined for total destruction. Once I made the choice to dedicate my life to follow Christ, once I started to study God's word and truly listen to what God was telling me through his word, the change continued. The closer I got to God the more I wanted to know about him. I felt as if a weight had been lifted, I started praising

God for a new beginning. If you would just open your heart and mind, to hear what God is saying to you, I promise you that you will feel a release from those strongholds that have you weighed down.

This is a book of
Poetry
Spoken word
Praise To God
Retaliation against Sin
Notification of What's
To come
Wake-up call to
What's going on
In the world
Today
And a warning to those
Non-believers
The ambiguous unclear
Uncertain
Cloudy, obscure
Confused
Misinformed

Minds of this
World
God is for real
And so is hell

The Word of God will always
Be my guide the words
That I write are a gift
From God, for without Him
I am nothing
I can do nothing
After much prayer as to what
I am to do with these writings
The scripture that God put on
My heart is

"Shout! A full-throated shout!
Hold nothing back-a trumpet-blast Shout!
Tell my people what's wrong with their lives
Face my family Jacob with their sins?"
Isaiah 58:1
(The Message)

"Cry aloud, spare not;
Lift your voice like trumpets
Tell my people their transgressions'
And the house of Jacob their sins"
Isaiah 58:1
(New King James)

Table of Contents

401 KINGDOM FUND

If you've listened and obeyed
If you've paid ten percent of your pay
Into the 401 kingdom fund
Where your interest grows
Night and day every day
No matter what goes on with
The rest of the world
The world may offer their
401 k plans but God
has the 401 kingdom fund
That's always safe and sound
It has the highest interest rate of return
You get everything you put in
At one hundred percent and then some
You can sleep in peace
No need to worry about your
Retirement home when the
Time comes you will be
Set on earth and eternally
Nobody but God can
Cancel it out
Bring it down
Wipe it out or cause it to crash
Praise be to God for my 401 Kingdom
fund

1

A Little While Longer

Times are harder
But God is stronger
Hold on just a little while longer
The battle is almost over
Soon a victory will be won
But until then we've got to
Press on just a little while longer
Be strong just a little while longer
Pray on just a little while longer
Hold on just a little while longer
We must hold on so we can do
What God wants and receive
What he has promised
God began a good work in us all
A long time ago although
We have all fallen from time to time
Hold on to the word of God
That has stood the test of time
Hold on when the mind
Seems weak
And lost
Press on when the world keeps trying to
Pull you apart
Pray on when there seems to be no light
For we must not become tired of doing

What is pleasing and good unto the Lord
For one day soon a harvest of eternal
Life will come to those
Who just hold on
A little while longer

BEFORE THE SHADOW COMES

Sisters/Brothers
I tell you once
I tell you twice
Once this life
Has ended its flight
No more songs to be sung
No more dances to be danced
No more cares of this life
Sisters/Brothers
Hear me Loud, and hear me now
Once the light of life is gone
No more songs to be sung
No more dances to be danced
I tell you once I tell you twice
While those gifts of God
Still Burn Bright inside you,
His Child
That he loved so much that he sent his
only son
To shed his blood to give you life
You need to let those gifts shine to
Give God the Honor and Glory,
God has given all his children

Gifts for the building of his kingdom so
Let those gifts shine for the whole world to
see
Before the shadow comes to end it all
For in the grave there will be
No dance
No song
No jobs to be done so give God the
Honor and
Glory before your day is done

Believe

Believe I do
I do believe
Believe I do
For all my being
Is in the believing
Of you O Lord

When I think back
On all the things I used
To do and how you brought
Me through........

I can't do anything but tell the world
How good and true you are
How knowing and believing in you
Will set them free to a new way of being

The mouth speaks the words that are in the
heart
With my heart I not only believe but I
trust you Lord
And I have faith in what you say
Though from time to time I have wavered
in my beliefs

Not my belief in you, O Lord
But in the belief that someone like me
could be so special to you
Me that child which no one really wanted
Could be worthy of your love and grace
A sinner such as I could be worthy of such
a love

Believe I do
I do believe
O Lord, how I do
Believe in you.

Cluttered minds

Cluttered Minds
Filled with chatter
Day in day out
So much technical jargon
Preoccupying our very being
Text messages ruling our time
Password after password
Constantly keeping our minds
Focused on everything but
The right things in this world
No time for the Word
No time for God too many
Text messages to
Read and send along
With all those
Passwords to try to
Memorize and hide
Preoccupation is the devil's
Creation to try to destroy God's
Creation don't allow technology
To preoccupy all your time
Remember to give God the creator of
All creation your time your mind and
Your heart as well

Daughters of Promise

Divas of a power
Not yet realized
Marvelously and uniquely made
Each one of you holding
A power inside
Not yet realized
Just waiting to be visualized

Each one of you have been
Filled with special gifts and talents
Just waiting to be visually and spiritually
Uplifting and enlightening to the world

Although you each have experienced
Your own uniquely different struggles
I implore you to keep moving forward
The past is the past
What's done is done

Forget and forgive, and let's move on
Just on the horizon, a new day is dawning
With each new morning, just keep on
rising to
A new way of thinking

A new way of being
A new way of living
A new way of loving
A new way of being loved
A new way of dealing with
Any future struggles

Look up to the Heavens
From whence cometh your help
Begin to utilize those gifts and
Talents hidden deep inside
Begin to realize and release the true Diva
Not the fake Diva the world chooses to
Glamorize but the Diva which represents
A heavenly power a
Devine Inspirationally Victoriously
Anointed
Sister

Embrace your future with enthusiasm
because
Enthusiasm encourages positive behavior
Know and realize you're not in this
journey alone
Embrace your mentor and the knowledge
she has

Seek her advice learn from her struggles
As you go through the struggles of your
life

Set your goals and surround yourself
With enthusiastic like-minded, uplifting,
Encouraging, spiritually connected Sisters

Daughters of Promise
Divas of a Power not
Not yet realized

Stand up and be counted
Know just how special you are
Let no one else tell you otherwise
Now go out there and show the
World just how special you are

Days Gone By

Looking back on days gone by
Thinking to myself
How on earth have we lived this long
Nobody but the Lord has kept us
Nobody but the Lord has brought us
This far to live this long safe from harm

I remember days of no car seats
Cars piled with folks two rows deep
No seatbelts required to drive a car
Riding my bike with no knee pads
Or helmets on having fun without a

Care in the world bumps and bruises
Here and there cleaned it, dressed it
Kept rolling right along still with
Out a care in the world playing
Outdoors all day long until the sun

Went down in the house before the
Street lights on or momma or daddy
At the house taking their belts off
Standing ready at the door to teach
Us responsibility and discipline

Stranger danger was unheard of
No strangers lived in the village
I came from, my village helped
To raise the children when I did
Wrong away from home the word of
It got home before I hit the door

Looking back on days gone by
How on earth have we lived this long
Nobody but the Lord has kept us
Nobody but the Lord has brought us
This far to live this long safe from harm

When momma said no, no meant no
No whining or caring on to get your way
When momma said yes you felt truly
blessed
Come Sunday morning we went to Sunday
School God came first no matter what

Each and every day of our lives
We were trained up right
In the sight of God
The Word was honored
And cherished in every house
Praise, worship and thanks

Flowing from every mouth
All on one accord
Respect and gratitude was on
Every mind no matter which
Village you came from

Looking back on days gone by
How on earth have we lived this long
Nobody but the Lord has kept us
Nobody but the Lord has brought us
This far to live this long safe from harm

Death Of A Race

Back in the day the KKK
Had and still does have a
Total disregard for human life
Especially the Negro life

Fear and ignorance fueled
Their hate for the Negro race
But history has flipped the script
Today the Gang Thugs
Have the same disregard

For not only the Negro race but
The whole human race in general
They are fueled by greed for the
Bling, Bling of gold and silver
Fine cars with spinners glistening

Day and night rap music blaring
Obscenities and thumping like the
Dinosaurs of Jurassic park busting caps
Night and day no matter who's in the way
In constant conflict and turmoil everyday

It used to be white against black but now

It's black against black we are doing
A genocide to our own race for the
Material things of this life a total disgrace
And disregard for the Negro race

Those that hate our race no longer have
To retaliate against us all they have to do
Is set back and watch us wipe out our own
Race one gang member at a time, one
drug
Dealer at a time one brother and sister at a
time

Designed by God

God's great design
Although I am black
Black by design
Matters not my color
All that matters is that
God loves and lives in me

I am beautiful
And I am black
I am a woman
I am a warrior
Yes that's me
Designed by God

A one of a kind design
Marvelously and wonderfully
Designed filled with many gifts
By God himself to be utilized
In God's own time

I am beautiful
And I am black
I am a woman
I am a warrior
I am designed by God

God's great design
If you don't like the
Way I look the
Color of my skin
 The texture of my hair
 The size of my lips

Then take it up with God
Because I am who I am
God's great design a one
Of a kind design

Each Day

Each day we rise
Each day we die
For God I'll live
Each day I rise
I thank you lord
For being justified
Just one day closer
To being glorified

No time to waste
No time to waste
Each day I wake
I thank the Lord
For one more day
To be sanctified

Each day we rise
Each day we die
For God I'll live
Each day I rise
I thank you lord
For being justified
Just one day closer
To being glorified

No time to waste
No time to waste
As a believer of
The word of God
I know to die
Is just the beginning

Each day we rise
Each day we die
For God I'll live
Each day I rise
I thank you lord
For being justified
Just one day closer
To being glorified

El Shaddai

Holy, Holy, Holy
El Shaddai
God Almighty
I thank you so much for loving me
A wretch marred by sin
Yet you sent a Savior in
To set me free from the sin
That I was in

Holy, Holy, Holy
El Shaddai
God Almighty
I thank you so much for loving me
When you saw there
Was no hope of me finding
My way out of the sin
That I was in

Holy, Holy, Holy
El Shaddai
God Almighty
I thank you once again
For sending a Savior
To set me free from the sin

That I was in

Holy, Holy, Holy
Elohim all power
Creator of Everything

Adonai, my Lord and Master
I give my all and all to you
Most Holy of Holy
El Shaddai

Finish Line

Almost at the finish line
Can't afford to stop now
Can't afford to be knocked off course
It's too late to turn back now
I love my life and my position with Christ
Though I've had many troubles in my life
My position in life with Christ
Has given me the strength to live this life
So now you see why I say
Can't afford to stop now
Can't afford to be knocked off course
Almost at the finish line

God's Word

God's word
His word is all you need to hear
When troubles and fear come near
His word is sound and true
And He's calling you to come hear
Not just when troubles near
But each and every day he wants
You to listen and hear what
He's telling you
God's thoughts toward you are
Always good no matter what you see
No matter what you hear
No matter what you've been through
He's testing you through the trials of life
To give you a future and a hope
God's word is all that you need to know
To deal with this crazy world
He never breaks His promises
He may not come exactly when
You want him to but I guarantee
He never breaks His promises
To those who love and obey His will
Communicate with God in prayer
Each and everyday
Get to know the Fathers Love

Hear what He is telling you
Trust and believe in His word
Way before trouble and fear come near
His word is sound and true
And He's calling you to come hear

Heart for Jesus

Fill your heart
With the love of Jesus

Make no room in your heart
For sin to visit

Allow no room for sin
To take hold give it all to Jesus

'Cause He's the only one
With the eternal vision

Invite Him into your heart today
I promise you won't be sorry

Just fill you heart
With the love of Jesus

I am a child of God

I am a child of God
I study the Word
God's word
In order to know
Right from wrong

I am a child of God
I study the Word
God's word
In order to know
Which way to go

I am a child of God
Can't nobody do me wrong
Cause I'm covered by his love

I am a child of God
As long as I follow
His Word
He'll keep me
Safe from harm

I am a Child of God
I may be young but
My faith is strong

Cause I'm grounded
In his Word
I am a child of God
I'm covered by his blood
He loved me so he died for me
To set me free from sin

I am a child Of God
I'll continue to study and
Believe in his Word
His words are my weapons
In times of trouble

I am a child of God
Heir to the Holy Kingdom
I'll do my best to live life right
To give my Father all the Glory

I am a child of God
No matter the Problem
I'll sing his Praises
For without him
I am nothing

I am a child of God
I know there is no other
Who loves me as much

As my Heavenly Father

Let all of us
The Children of God
Who Truly Love Him
Stand and lift our hands
To applaud and give
Our Father
Total Praise and
Thanks for all
He has done for us.

I Am Beautiful

I am beautiful
And I am black
I am a woman
I am a warrior
Yes that's me
Designed by God

God's great design
A strong mighty
Fierce woman am I
Designed to do great things
For the good of the kingdom
To give God the Glory

I am beautiful
And I am black
I am a woman
I am a warrior
Yet that's me
Designed by God

God's great design
Designed to love
Designed to bear fruit
To pass on the love

Designed to tell the
World of the Holy one's love

I am beautiful
And I am black
I am a woman
I am a warrior
Yes that's me

I hear you, Lord

Loud and clear, I hear you
Even when I didn't want to I heard you
You've been calling me since I was young
I realize now I am a chosen one
You chose me before I was born
You came and rescued me while I was
Sinking deep in sin
You threw me a line and pulled me out
Of that sin I was sinking in
Through your word I know now that
You'd already planned a long time ago
That I'd be among the chosen ones
To carry out your word to the world
With these gifts you've given me
I hear you loud and clear I hear you Lord
I shall carry this light you've given me
And I shall let it shine bright to be a guide
Out of darkness for someone else
Matters not who or when
All that matters is that I am
Obedient and let this light bestowed in me
Shine to guide someone out of the
darkness
To give you the Glory to pass on the Love

To lead another soul out of the darkness
to
Show them the power source which will
light
Their power to lead someone from the
darkness

I look to you, O God

I look to you, O God on high
To be my one true guide
Before I accepted you into my life
I was blinded by worldly desires
Blinded to what was good and true
Blinded by greed, glitz, and glamour
Fulfilling my desires was all I knew

I look to you, O God on high
To be my one true guide
Before you came and rescued me
I lived in total darkness
Totally unaware that there is where
I would stay for all eternity if you had
Not come and rescued me

I look to you, O God on high
To be my one true guide
No longer am I blinded by worldly desires
I see the truth more clearly now
Your words I hear when true disciples are
near
When shepherds who do your will, speak
your words

To fill my spirit full of your loving
lifesaving words

I look to you, O God on high
To be my one true guide
I eagerly wait to hear from you
Each and every day I rise, thanking you
For each day I'm allowed to be alive
Searching high to know your will and
Ways, your desire for my life

I look to you, O God on high
To be my one true guide
Feeling your love, mercy, and grace
Surrounding me each and everyday
Longing to know the God who loves
Me no matter what I do or how bad
My life looks you love me no matter what

I look to you, O God on high
To be my one and only guide
Longing to see your glory upon my life
At the end of my life's journey but until
Then I shall continue to let my light shine
For all to see how great your love can be
When they put their life and trust in you

In My Face

In my face
Day and night
Night and day
Round the clock
A sentry sets ready
And waiting everywhere
I turn inside outside
Flicking through the channels
Ready to shove it in my face
Everywhere I look it
Beckons me to take a look
Jingles blaring here and there
Smells that make you
Quiver and shake with thoughts
Oh just how great it would be
To sample a little bit just a bit
To slow the shivers & shakes
Listen up as you talk to yourself
Telling yourself you'll
Worry about the weight tomorrow
Just a taste just a taste
To get it out of my face

It's Time

It's time for us to
To stop the violence
Stop the crying
Stop the denying and
Start relying on God's Word
As we were told a long time ago

The word of God
Has always been our weapon
Of defense in times of trouble
And Lord, we as a people
Have seen our share of troubles

Open your eyes and see what
Is happening to our children today
What has happened to the teachings of
Our past, when did we decide
To not heed Gods word?

From the 1st Century to the
21st century we still continue to
Disobey God's Word,
We've gone from wondering in
The desert because of disobedience

To our children dying in the streets
because
We've chosen to go against God's
teachings
As we were told a long time ago

Although many of us
Are trying to live the right way
By obeying God's Word many others
Are not and O Lord, what a
Heavy price we all are paying

So many of God's children young and old
are
Disrespectful, disobedient, cruel,
unthankful, unholy,
Blasphemers, lovers of money and material
possessions,
Unloving, unforgiving, slanderers without
self-control,
Brutal despisers of God. Traitors against
their own family
Head strong, haughty lovers of pleasure
Rather than lovers of God.

It's time for us to
Stop the violence

Stop the crying
Stop denying and
Start relying on God's Word
As we were told a long time ago

You see if you had of
Stayed in God's Word
As the old folks told us a long time ago
We would already have known
About these times we are living in today
God's Word has always been there
To warn us of danger
Everything we need to know is and
Has always been in the scriptures
If you turn to Second Timothy
Chapter Three and read verse
One through four
It tells you what the people will
Be like in the end days.
Just think how different it might have
been for
Some of God's Children who are hurting
and crying
Over all the violence and the loss of loved
ones
Who have died senseless deaths because
they

Chose not to obey God's Word
How many of them might still be alive
Today.

Proverbs 22:6
Train up a child in the way he should go
And when he is old he will not depart from
it

Mark 10:15
Assuredly I say to you, whoever does not
Receive the Kingdom of God as a little
child
Will by no means enter it."

1Corinthians 13:11
When I was a child, I spoke as a child, I
understood
As a child, I thought as a child; but when I
became
A man, I put away childish things.

**We have taken away our children's youth
By exposing them to far too many
Adult things because it looked cute, or
impressive**

Nothing is sacred anymore. The enemy
the deceiver, the father of lies
Has blinded us into believing it is all just
fun and entertainment
Witchcraft, Magicians, vampires, spells, the
Children today know more about the
things of darkness
Than the things of
Our Heavenly Father

2 Timothy 3:15
And that from childhood you have known
the
Holy scriptures which are able to make
you wise for
Salvation through Faith which is in Christ
Jesus

Look at what our children are doing today
in the world
Look how we have failed them by not
obeying God's Word
Many do not even know who Jesus is
They have no respect for any one
Lost souls are wondering in the desert
Of life with no sense of direction
Not knowing who they really are

Or what they should be doing with
Their lives how many more will die
because
Of our disobedience

Kingdom Builder

I am a Kingdom Builder
I don't need a hammer
I don't need a nail
All I need is Jesus Christ
And the word of God
To do my job for the
Glory of God
To fulfill the building
Of God's Holy Kingdom
As a Kingdom builder

My mission is to
Magnify
The Lord at
All times to

Multiply
The number
Of souls saved
For the Holy Kingdom
Grow them up in the
Wisdom and word of God
So they too can

Minister

To the lost souls of the world
Fulfilling the Great Commission
As proclaimed by God
Spreading the good news of His
Love around the world for all
To make the choice to be saved
To one day live eternally in
Gods Holy Kingdom

Let Him In

Don't you know that God is
Waiting on you to
Let Him into your life
Let Him into your Mind
Let Him into your heart
Let Him into your house
Not just on Sunday morning
But Monday through Sunday
And every day of your life?
Don't you know that?
In order for everything to turn
Out right in your life
You've got to let Him into your life
You've got to fight the fight to be holy
By staying in the face of the Father
Every day and every night
Fasting and praying and
Studying His word daily
The battle won't be easy
For the enemy the evil one
Is on his job daily seeking to kill
Steal and destroy you
Your life
Your mind
Your heart

And everyone in your house
But if you hold on tight
Let God cover you with His
Love, Grace and Mercy and
Be not conformed to this world but
Allow God to transform you by the
renewing
Of your mind with His word
Let Him In
Let Him In
Let Him into all of your life
And watch how God will make a difference
in your
Life that will make you wonder why it
took you so long to let Him into your life.

LET NOT YOUR HEART BE TROUBLED

Verse-(Soprano)
If you've heard my words
If you believe and trust
Then
Let not your heart be troubled
For I am with you

Verse-(Alto)
No matter what you're going through
Just call on me and I'll be there for you
So
Let not your heart be troubled
For I am with you

Verse-(Tenor)
And when the time comes
For you to come home
To that place I've prepared
I'll receive you, that where I am
You may be

Everybody-(Unison)
Let not your heart be troubled
For I am with you
I'm by your side both day & night
My child
I've always been and always will
Be until the end of time
Oh, oh
Until the end of time

Let Not Your Heart Be Troubled
Version#2

You may feel like you're alone
But know I've always been there
I knew you before you were born
I've been waiting for you to call on me
Waiting for you to call my name
Waiting for you to see the truth
And know that I am your Father
Let not your heart be troubled
For I am with you
I'm by your side both day and night
My child
I've always been and always will be
Until the end of time
Oh yes
Until the end of time

Letter to My Father

Father God
You see us day in day out
You see how we fuss left and right
About so many things in this life

You see how we make and put
Things that really are not all
That important at the head of
Our lives before you, Dear Father

Our careers that you blessed us with
Achievements that we could have never
Achieved without you in our lives
Our life activities we find more

Important than spending time with you
In prayer and worship, fellowshipping
With our sisters and brothers coming
Together to give you praise, Honor and
Glory

Yet Father in the midst of all our
Disobedience you still give us Grace and
Mercy

By allowing us each day to see another new
day
Yet we your creation the ones that you
sent your

One and only son to shed his blood for
the sake
Of our salvation to free us from sin
We can't even take the time to simply say
Thank you Father, O Lord God for that.

I am truly sorry, sorry that many of my
sisters
And brothers are so ungrateful,
unappreciative
Unwilling to share their lives with you
many
Are even doubtful that you even exist

You are our Father the creator of all that
we are
You're the one who keeps us safe from
dangers seen
And unseen Lord God I am sorry that
many of my
Sisters and brothers are not as close to you

As they need to be, but I myself do
appreciate
All that you do have done and are going
To do, in my life. There have been so
Many times when you should have walked

Away and left me crawling, through all the
Messes I made in my life but by your
Grace
And Mercy you picked me up, brushed me
Off and started me on my way again yet

Each time I've fallen you've answered my
calling
Each time I've fallen it has made me
stronger
Each time I've made a mistake
Each time I've struggled
Each time
Each time
Each time, Father

It has always been you who has brought
me through
It has always been you to comfort me
When the tears start to falling, Thank you
Thank you Heavenly Father for loving me
Through all my good times and bad
Thank you
Father

LIFES MOMENTS

A moment can slip by in the blink of an
eye
A moment can seem to last for an eternity
A moment can set the stage for the rest
Of your life
Think for a moment
About some of the moments in your life

In that moment of giving birth
You thought it would never be over

In that moment of passion and pleasure
You prayed it would last forever
But
In that moment did you stop to think
about
The many consequences of life's
moments?

In that moment of anger when you lost
Total control and you did or said
Some things you should not have

In that moment of passion and pleasure
You now have pain in your life that
You never took the time to think about

You see life's moments can carry some
Heavy consequences so please take
A moment out and talk to God about it
Before you make a life changing decision
That could change
The rest of the moments of your life

Listen up

Listen Up
People of the world
God is trying to tell you something
Be wise not to waste your lives
Chasing after the material things
Keeping up with the worldly ways
Yet oblivious to the word of God
Be on guard for the night is almost over
Position and power shall pass away
No matter the amount of money
You've saved you can't buy your
Way into the pearly Gates
Of Heaven

Move Me

Move me outta' my way, Lord
Move me outta' my way

So I can do what you want me to
So I can do your will

Remove that part of me Lord
That tries to rebel

Remove that part of me
That keeps fighting your will

O Lord this battle within
Just keeps on battling, oh

Move me outta' my way, Lord
So I can do your will

The New Jerusalem

It's coming,
It's coming
The New Jerusalem
The Nations of the saved
Shall walk in the light
Illuminated by
God Almighty
And His Son
The Lamb of God
No need for the Moon or the Sun
In the New Jerusalem
No need for Denominations
Holy Temples or Mega Churches
'Cause the Lord
God Almighty
And His Son
The Lamb of God
Will be
The Sun the Moon
And all the Holy Temples
And Mega Churches we'll ever
Need
In the New Jerusalem

No Not You

So many of us live our lives in an
emotional haze
Never feeling worthy of anything good
decent or
Exciting happening to us allowing the
world to control
Our ups and downs based on what mood
or fad is going
On in the world at that particular time.

No matter how hard we try always giving it
our all and all
Yet the world keeps saying
No, No, Not you
No, No, No Way No How,
Wearing our feelings on our sleeves
allowing the
World to pull our emotional strings giving
into what
The world ordains and not what God is
saying to us

When I think back on how many times
I've been
Pushed away pushed aside rejected
neglected put
Down laughed at told by the world I'm not
pretty
Enough light enough skinny enough
smart enough
Never given a real reason why I'm not
good enough

The many tears I've shed because of the
No, No, Not you
No, No, No Way No How's
That has been spoken during my lifetime
Until the day I heard Christ calling me to
change
My life to start living with the purpose He
designed
Me for once I opened my mind to hear
God's Word

And to feel His love that had always been
there
But I was too busy trying to please the
world who

Had no love for me personally once I
chose to follow
Christ Jesus the
No, No, Not you
No, No, No Way No How's
Didn't hurt no more they meant nothing
for
In Christ He made me for a particular
reason
My steps are ordered by God to be used by
Him in His time what He has for me is for
me
The world may say
No, No, Not you
No, No, No way no how
But God has the final
Say no matter what
The world may say

Save the Children #1

Save the children
Look around and see them
They are crying for you to see them
The them they really are
Not the them you think they are
God's Word says the children are the
Center of life in the kingdom
If we do not know God's Word then
How can we really know how important
Our children really are
We substitute Love and Time
With gimmicks and toys
 Games material bliss so they
 Won't miss the you they desperately
Want to know unhappy children grow
Up to be unhappy adults. The Word
Of God says to train up a child in the
Way they should go yet each and
Every day another child lay dying in
The streets or they are committing
Suicide, always looking for ways
To escape reality to escape the pain
Of you not seeing the them they really are
Many gave up on your love a long time
ago

And started looking for love in all the
wrong
Places babies having babies or in too many
cases
There are other adults waiting to teach
them wrong
Kinds of teachings. Oh please look at our
children
We the parents to the greatest gift known
to mankind
We the parents of our future kind
We the parents who are so busy trying save
a dime
We the parents trying to elevate to the
highest part of the establishment.
The high cost of fame and fortune is the
loss of really getting to know
Love and nurture our children the way the
Word tells us to.
So please wake up and see them for they
are our future

Save the Children #2

Save the children
See them big and small
Crying for your attention
Desiring to know and feel your love

See them as they really are
Not the them you think they should be
Innocent from birth like a white canvas
'Till we do the things we do to them

Like a vicious cycle repeating itself
Over and over again and again
For what we sow into them
We shall surely reap from them

Hurt children grow up to be hurt adults
Sad children grow up to be sad adults
Angry children grow up to be angry adults
Confused children grow up to be confused
adults
Mean spirited children grow up to be mean
spirited adults
Cruel children grow up to be cruel adults

If we teach them unhealthy habits

They grow up to be unhealthy adults
But then again parents only teach what
they know
The Word of God says train up a child in
the way
He should go, when we stopped teaching
the
Word of God that is when all the problems
began
Spiritually dysfunctional
Not believing in
Biblically dysfunctional

Not knowing the Word of God
Not studying the Word of God
Not teaching the Word of God
Not practicing the Word of God
Not heeding the Word of God

Leads to
Dysfunctional families
Open to every spirit that comes along
No sense of direction of right or wrong
Lost in a maze of worldly desires and
distractions

In many cases this has
Created, caused, and developed
Dysfunctional children that grow
Into dysfunctional adults
Which has led to so many negative
lifestyles
Low self-esteem, disconnect from society
Gangs, drugs, prostitution, serial type
behaviors,

When children feel no one cares
Why should they care about themselves?
Or anyone else
When children feel no one sees
The pain they feel inside
Suicide, homicide, drug addiction, self-
destruction
Anything to get someone's attention,
your attention

Because they hurt and do not have
The family love and support as they desire
Many of our children feel the only way to
get
The love they so desire the feeling
someone cares

Is to join a gang filled with hate and
violence

In which we all end up paying a price either
Three hots and a cot, or we become the
victims
Of all that hate and violence built up from
years
Of hurt, anger, lack of attention, and lack
of love
For what we all sow into them is what we
shall reap

If we teach them hate we get hate
If we teach them prejudice we get prejudice
If we teach them greed we get greed
If we teach them to lie we get liars
If we teach them to steal we get thieves
But if we go back to the scriptures
Biblical teachings of God
If we teach them love we get love
If we teach them peace we get peace
If we teach them respect we get respect
If we teach them courage we get courage
If we teach them forgiveness we get
forgiveness

If the Military can take our young men
and women
And teach them to be lean mean
honorable respectful
Killing machines, then why is it so hard
for us
To teach innocent little babies how to
grow up to
Love, and respect one another as God loves
us
Maybe, just maybe if we did there would
Be no need for the Military because there
Would be
No war
No violence
No discord
No hate
See the children who grow into adults
See them big and small
Crying for your attention
Desiring to know and feel love

Slow Down

Slow down and look to that which
God has truly blessed you with.
We live in a world where everyone
Is in a hurry to do everything
Have more
Do more
Eat more

So focused on the future
Can't enjoy the present
Always focused on the
Next phase of your life
The young are always in a
Hurry to be grown
To have more
Do more
Eat more

Never slowing down
To enjoy the true joys
Of family & friends
The present time
Of life.

Open your eyes and see
The blessings God has
Bestowed upon you
We get so caught up
In outdoing
Having more trying
To empress others
With material possessions
That we lose sight of what
Is really important
Is not the human life more
Important than material
Possessions?

For we are all here today
And gone tomorrow
It's not wrong to desire to have
Nice things but when you start
Acting as if you are better or
Thinking you are better than those
Who have less than you

When you start pushing away from Family
And friends simply because they do not
Have what you have been blessed with
Worse when you start turning your back
on God

When your possessions become what you
worship
So if you have been
Blessed to have more than someone else
You better stop and think about
Where your blessings come from

So what if you don't have
A fortune or a big fine
Fancy ego car
Matters not if you do or don't
Once you die you won't be
Able to do anything but leave
It behind
All your money you have strived
To gain by way of working
Your fingers to the bone
Or maybe by doing a few dishonest
Things walking on the dark side
For the gain of material things
That is simply here today and gone
Tomorrow
Slow down and take a look
At that which
You should deem as really important

So Many times

Many Times
I think to myself how
I wish I could run from it all
All the ups and downs of life
Expectations disappointments all those
falls

Wish God would let me hide
Until he calls us home to be with him
Sometimes I get so frustrated with life
All the decisions and choices afraid I'll
make

The wrong choices not sure if I am hearing
Correctly what I should do scared to make
A move don't want to make a mistake and
Disappoint God or my family in any way
But then again where shall I run nowhere
To go only two choices to choose from
Either live my life to the fullest with faith

In the Lord without fear after all children
of
God have no fear or I could die never
trying
Never living giving up throwing in the
towel
Don't want to die nowhere to run got to
stay
The course praying to God with all my
heart
That I make the right choices please God
please
 Help me to make the right choices in my
life
Please God please.

To The Fallen Young

To the fallen young
Dying by the hand
Of street violence
Dead and gone no
More to rise to
See a new day's
Dawn gone are the
Years of your life
Before your time
Never taught in the
Way of wisdom
Never reaching your
Full potential lost
On the way to
Salvation's reward
Lost to the darkness
For ever more never
To rise again to see
Another day's light
For ever gone to the
Dark side of eternity
The fallen young dead
And gone no more to
Rise a wise son makes
A glad father but

A foolish son is
The grief of his
Mother

The Foot Steps of God

The footsteps of God
Can be heard all around the world
The countdown has begun
Listen to the cries of the people
From around the world
The many tears and sorrows that
Emerge with each new tomorrow
The wind and the waves know Gods power
Tornados, tsunamis, earthquakes and fires
Of biblical proportions
Causing much destruction all around the
world

The footsteps of God
Can be heard all around the world
Drawing closer and closer
Unusual forms of viruses
So much hate and violence with each
New tomorrow unlike any seen before
Behold and know the mighty power of
God
As His footsteps draw closer and closer
To the true Christian followers
The ones who have taken the time to
Build a personal relationship with God

And have made the choice to follow
And obey Gods Word, you know

The footsteps of God
Can be heard all around the world
Drawing closer and closer
Those of you who have studied God's
Word know that this is not our home
That we are but strangers in a strange land
Passing through
And although those footsteps
Appear to be getting closer and closer
We still have a job to do we must continue
Our mission fulfilling God's commission
To make disciples until God says we're
done

His footsteps are a reminder of the mighty
And awesome power He holds in his hands
Know that God is the creator of all our
Yesterdays, todays and tomorrows
Those of you who have taken the time to
get
To know God by spending time with Him
in
Prayer, study and meditation
You know that He loves us and

That the plans He has for us are for good
And not for evil to give us all who believe
a
Future and a hope
All that we go through here is just a test
Of our faith in the
Lord our God

The You I See

As I look around at all the sights
And sounds of the world today
I'm trying to understand why so many
Can't see the you I see, O Lord
Your word
O Lord I've come to know
More and more each day
(<u>Inspires</u>)?
my heart to write these words
To let the world know
The you that I have come to know

So they can see the awesome and
Mighty you I see
Although Your Word tells me in
First Timothy chapter four verse one
(1 Timothy 4:1)
That in the end times many will depart
From the faith giving heed to deceiving
spirits
And doctrine of demons
These being the things of the dark side
Which we see continually in society being
Paraded across screen and stage

For all the world to see and hear
To glamorize and fantasize about
Witches warlocks vampires sorcerers
Magicians misleading the world to believe
That these things are just a bit of fun
If only the world would take the time
To open their minds to Your Word and
hear

The truth they would know that in
Deuteronomy chapter eighteen verse ten
and twelve
(Deuteronomy 18:10-12)
Says for all who deal with magic sorcerers
witchcraft
That those things of the dark side are and
abomination
To you O Lord
The you O Lord I have come to know and
Love why can't they see the you I see the
one who
Gives us the word of truth if we just
believe and trust
He will show us right from wrong
Yet the world still continues to live this life
morally wrong
Continuing to do those things

That are and abomination to you O Lord
Insisting it is all

Just a bit of entertainment just a little fun
to pass the time
Do they know what they are waiting on as
they are passing the time
Where do they think they are going after
such time has passed by
If you live in darkness among death and
destruction then it stands
To reason that it is a place you long to be
in, that is
Where you find your happiness
Where you choose your eternal resting
place to be
Living among those things of the dark
side
Living among mere illusion
Those things you've put before God
The God of Light not Darkness
The God of Life not Death

Second Timothy chapter three verses two
thru five
(2Timothy 3:2-5)

Tells us about the kind of times we are
living in today
O Lord if the people of the world could
only open their hearts and
Minds to know Your Word
The Word which tells of everlasting love
and life
That tells us exactly how to
Live this life
The things I see in the world today
Tattoos on many souls from head to toe
The young and the old in total disregard
To Your Word O Lord

Leviticus chapter nineteen verses twenty
eight
(Leviticus 19:28)
Would set them straight on what is right
and wrong
If they would just open up their hearts and
minds
To Your Word then they would know
their
Bodies are sacred temples
Not walking bill boards of unusual designs
It has been said that it is what you don't
know

That can hurt you
I pray that those who have heard or read
these words
Will want to hear more of Your Words
Of Truth O Lord
The Holy Bible is filled with all you need to
know
In order to live this life right
Someone once said the Bible is the

B-asic

I-nstructions

B-efore

L-eaving

E-arth

To God Be the Glory of the
Hearing of these words.

Traffic

My signal's blinking
My signal's blinking
Can't they see that?
My turn signal's blinking
Look to my left
Look to my right
All I see is road
Rage glares on
Every face
Gas prices causing much
Of their facial stress and strife
Cell phones locked on the
Sides of almost every face
With no concern of my plight
I'm locked in tight
Got to get off at the next right
Gave my signal a mile ago
Still no release
Two more miles to go
Until my exit comes in sight
Maybe someone will let me go
Yet I see not a courteous soul
On the road
Have to go with the flow

Maybe some kind soul
Will let me go
My signal's blinking
My signal's blinking
Where have all the kind souls gone
Can't they see my turn signal's on

Truly, Truly

Shake 'em up
Wake 'em up
Shake 'em up
Wake 'em up

Let me tell you what
It's really all about
Either you are
Or you aren't
Trying to live a Christian way of life

Truly, truly I say unto you
Truly, truly it's okay to be young
Truly, truly it's okay to have fun

But
There comes a point where even the
Young need to take a stand for what's
decent and right
Time for you to make up your mind which
side your you're on
Heaven or Hell
It's time to roll on

Because you're grown you gotta make a
choice

Truly I say unto you
Truly, truly it's okay to be young
Truly, truly it's okay to have fun

But
I believe it's time for you to take
A look at your situation and ask yourself
If you are really living a Christian way of
life--are you?
Sitting in the presence of all that is Godly,
are you?
Walking a Godly way of life, are you?
Standing for all the Godly-good things in
life?
Are you living your life in the center of
God's Love?
Are you embracing all the biblical
knowledge that God
Is making available to you or are you
living your life on the
Edge of nothingness---just going through
the motions on Sunday
Mornings looking like you think a
Christian ought to look

Some of you sing in the choir fall out and
shout Hallelujah
But do you really know what it's really all
about
Truly, truly I say unto you
Truly, truly it's okay to be young
Truly, truly it's okay to have fun

But
Somehow you've gotten confused and
thought
You were only supposed to look the part
Of a Christian not act the part of a
Christian
You've never truly embraced Gods Word
 'Cause

You've just been going through the
motions
You've never truly communicated with
God unless
You are in a bind with no way out
You've just been going through the
motions
You've never taken the time to ask God
what

His will is for your life
You've just been going through the
motions
You've refused to make God the center of
Attention because you are too busy trying
to
Be the center of attention
You're just going through the motions

Truly, truly I say unto you
Truly, truly it's okay to be young
Truly, truly it's okay to have fun

But
Having fun doesn't mean you have to
Have a worldly mentality filled with
All sorts of perverted sexual sinning
Letting evil thoughts control you
Being rude, crude drunken fools is
Not the will of God for your life yes
You may only live once but what if
That night of just having fun turned
Out to be your last night on earth
Of just having fun what will you say
When your maker comes
Yes, being a Christian is very hard
To do when you're young and just

Want to have fun because the world is
Always pulling at you
The sin whisperer, the deceiver,
The enemy is always there ready
To teach you a new thing or two
You will always be tempted by
Non-believers both family and
Friends to turn your back on God.
Stay strong take a stand for God
Take time to sit with God
In order for you to be able to
Do the will of God
Be Blessed

Wanna' Walk This Walk

Well I'm
Gonna' do right in my life with God
Gonna' give Him my all and all
Now that I've been justified
I'm working to be sanctified
Gonna' Walk this walk with Christ
Until I'm glorified with God

Well I
Know this journey's gonna' be hard
'Cause Satan's gonna' try and stop my walk
Through whatever means he can
Satan wants me to join him in hell for all
eternity

Never to reach my glorification up in
heaven with my Lord
Satan knows the things that hold me
bound
He knows what buttons to push to lock
me down

He'll use my family
He'll use my friends and even
Some so called Christians
To try to stop me
To try to block me

O Lord I'm gonna' walk this walk with you
Until the day of my glorification

We've got to take a Stand

It is time for us the followers of the Way
The disciples of God us Christians walking
In the light with the light in us
To be the light stand and take a stand
We've got to stand up for God's truth
We've got to stop playing church
We've got to start practicing God's Word
daily
Not just on Sunday morning

We've got to start living for what we
believe
We've got to live for the Word and not
the world
We've got to live and be more like Christ
It's time for us to get back to the basics in
life
It's time for us to get down to the business
of
Practicing what we teach and preach in this
life
Trusting what God is telling us through
His Word
Even when everything around us is
looking rough

We've got to take a stand
We've got to be the light stand
We've got to stop playing church
We've got to start living this walk right
It is time to stop playing games
It is time for us to stop frontin'
In the name of Jesus

It ain't gonna' work no more
No it ain't gonna' work no more
Time is really running out
This ain't no joke without a doubt
Time is really running out
It's time for us to shine the light
God has placed within
All His true disciples
It's time to be the light for the world
To lead them out of the darkness
It's time to take a stand for life and
What's right and true in Christ

When Jesus Comes

Have you ever thought about
Whatcha' gonna' be doing
When he comes?
Whatcha' gonn'a be doing
When he comes?

Will you be busy working for the Lord
Side by side with your
Christian brothers and sisters
Helping to build the kingdom large?
Whatcha' gonna' be doing
When he comes?

Or are you among those who have
Only been concerned about your own
Selfish desires and wants no time
to Know the will of God?
Whatcha' gonna' be doing
When he comes?

Will you be praising and worshiping
Him with a song and a dance?
Will you be praising him with the
Harp or instrument of choice?
Whatcha' gonna' be doing
When he comes?

Or have you spent all lifetime chasing
After fame and fortune forsaking any
And everything to secure your fortune?
Whatcha' gonna' be doing
When he comes?

Will he find you on your knees praying
For lost souls, praying for your family
Praying for peace on earth?
Whatcha' gonna' be doing
When he comes?

Or will he find you in a back alley
Shooting up on drugs selling drugs,
Killing for drugs, stealing for drugs
Committing sexual lude acts for drugs?
Whatcha' gonna 'be doing
When he comes?

Will you be ready when he comes?
Have you obeyed the Laws of God?
Will you be rejoicing and praising
When the time comes to claim the
throne?
Whatcha' gonna' be doing
When he comes?

Or are you that scholar Suma Qum Laude
All knowing intellectual who has believed
In everything from witches and warlocks
But not the God who created you?
Whatcha 'gonna' be doing
When he comes?

I pray to God you who have ignored God
for
So long you will indeed wake-up and see
your
Wrong before your time is all gone.
Time is running out.
Whatcha 'gonna' be doing
When he comes?

Elise Lorraine Shelbourne Chambers-Walker

Child of God
Poet, Writer, Actress, Artist, Voice Over, Ambassador to the Kingdom, Wife, Mother& Grand Mother

Born Elise Lorraine Shelbourne Chambers on May 1, 1958 and raised in Shelbyville, Kentucky.   Elise was raised by a housekeeper, a beautician, and a very strict and stern disciplinarian School Teacher, who later went back to school and became a Social Worker.   Elise started writing at a very early age as a way of expressing her feelings. Being very shy and soft spoken she was bullied by many of her peers in school, writing and drawing were her way of escaping her reality while growing up. Her birth mother gave her up before she was a year old, but over the next two years after abandoning Elise her mother went on to give birth to two more children which she did raise herself.

Never quite feeling like she was wanted or fit in. The one person that she truly felt loved her unconditionally was the woman she called mother, Mamie Mickey the housekeeper.   Mamie died in 2005 at the age of 100, she was a proverbs woman. Mamie introduced Elise to God at a very early age at the old Clay Street Baptist Church, under the leadership of the Rev. Claude Taylor. Mamie was a close friend of the family who had one child a son who died before he was a year old. Mamie and Elise's great Aunt Arletta the beautician were best friends, Mamie desired to raise Elise as her own child, so Arletta and her sister Helen the Social Worker agreed to allow her to do so. They were there to financially help to support and teach Elise. Helen was the overseer of almost everything the child did. Many times Mamie and Helen would clash as to what was best for her. Elise's journey has been long and sometimes physically and emotionally rough, but God has always blessed her in many ways.

Elise is married to her childhood sweetheart Fred D. Walker for thirty five years they have three children; Christopher, Kimberly, April. She is the grandmother of seven; Alexis, Michael Jr, Regan, Jaden, Andre Jr., Gabrielle, Kaden and she has two new grand babies on the way. She is very proud to be the mother-in-law to Vanessa, Andre Sr., Sam. Elise is a member of the Canaan Christian Church in Louisville, KY. She has been a member for almost ten years she is a Christ centered, passionate, connected and committed Christian on assignment to use the gifts God has given her for the Kingdom.